D0772679

Tornadoes

by Grace Hansen

Abdo **WEATHER** Kids

abdopublishing.com

Published by Abdo Kids, a division of ABDO, PO Box 398166, Minneapolis, Minnesota 55439.

Printed in the United States of America, North Mankato, Minnesota.

052015

092015

 THIS BOOK CONTAINS
RECYCLED MATERIALS

Photo Credits: AP Images, iStock, Shutterstock, © EPG_EuroPhotoGraphics p.17 / Shutterstock.com

Production Contributors: Teddy Borth, Jennie Forsberg, Grace Hansen

Design Contributors: Laura Rask, Dorothy Toth

Library of Congress Control Number: 2014958556

Cataloging-in-Publication Data

Hansen, Grace.

Tornadoes / Grace Hansen.

   p. cm. -- (Weather)

ISBN 978-1-62970-935-2

Includes index.

1. Tornadoes--Juvenile literature.   I. Title.

551.55--dc23

                  2014958556

Table of Contents

A Tornado

A tornado is a very strong wind.

You can see a tornado. It is

long and thin. It spins very fast.

4

5

Thunderclouds

All tornadoes form from **thunderclouds**. But not all thunderclouds make tornadoes.

6

Air near the ground must be warm and **humid**. The air above it is cold and dry. When the two meet, the warm air shoots up. This makes a **thundercloud**.

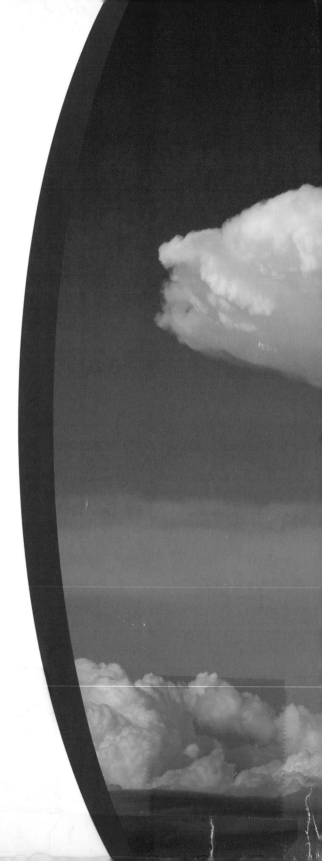

9

Funnel Clouds

Wind blows in the storm. The air inside the cloud spins. The spinning can make a funnel cloud. If it touches the ground, it is a tornado.

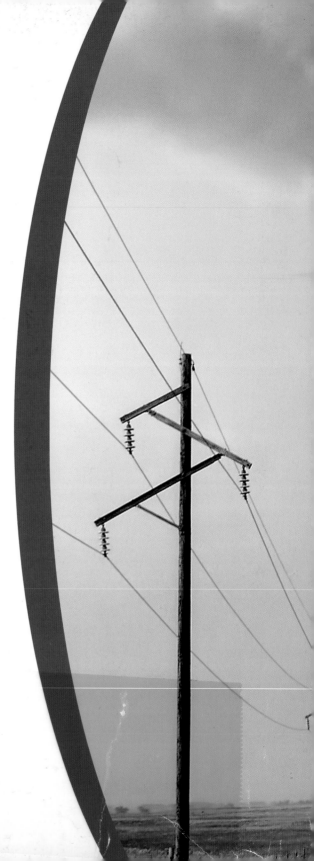

11

Touchdown

A tornado's path is usually 100 yards (91 m) long. It usually lasts for about 10 minutes. But it can move farther and last longer.

13

Scientists have a special scale.

It is called the Enhanced Fujita

Scale (EF-Scale). The EF-Scale

rates a tornado's strength.

EF-SCALE

SCALE	EF	WIND SPEED
	0	65-85 MPH / 105-137 KM/H
	1	86-110 MPH / 138-178 KM/H
	2	111-135 MPH / 179-218 KM/H
	3	136-165 MPH / 219-266 KM/H
	4	166-200 MPH / 267-322 KM/H
	5	OVER 200 MPH / OVER 322 KM/H

The weakest tornado is an EF-0. Over half of all tornadoes are EF-0s. Some branches may break off trees. Some homes may need a little repair.

The strongest tornadoes are EF-4s and EF-5s. These make up about 8 percent of all tornadoes. Cars fly through the air. Homes are destroyed.

Tornado Safety

Find a safe place in case of a tornado. A basement is the best place. A small closet is the next best spot. Always stay away from windows.

How a Tornado Forms

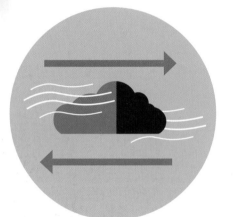

Wind blows
in a storm

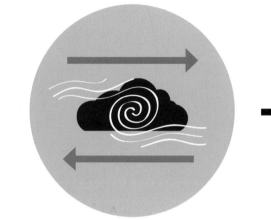

Opposite winds create
spinning inside a
thundercloud

A funnel cloud
drops from the
thundercloud. It
touches **down to**
become **a tornado**

22

Glossary

Enhanced Fujita Scale (EF-Scale) – a scale that is used to measure the strength of a tornado based on the damage it caused.

humid – containing a high amount of water or water vapor.

thundercloud – a large, electrically charged cloud that often creates thunderstorms and tornadoes.

Index

abdokids.com

Use this code to log on to abdokids.com and access crafts, games, videos, and more!

Abdo Kids Code:
WTK9352